PLANT POWER

PRICKLY PLANTS

by Mari Schuh

pogo

Ideas for Parents and Teachers

Pogo Books let children practice reading informational text while introducing them to nonfiction features such as headings, labels, sidebars, maps, and diagrams, as well as a table of contents, glossary, and index.

Carefully leveled text with a strong photo match offers early fluent readers the support they need to succeed.

Before Reading

- "Walk" through the book and point out the various nonfiction features. Ask the student what purpose each feature serves.
- Look at the glossary together. Read and discuss the words.

Read the Book

- Have the child read the book independently.
- Invite him or her to list questions that arise from reading.

After Reading

- Discuss the child's questions. Talk about how he or she might find answers to those questions.
- Prompt the child to think more. Ask: What prickly plants have you seen? Where were they? What kinds of animals or insects do you think they were defending themselves against?

Pogo Books are published by Jump!
5357 Penn Avenue South
Minneapolis, MN 55419
www.jumplibrary.com

Library of Congress Cataloging-in-Publication Data

Names: Schuh, Mari C., 1975- author.
Title: Prickly plants / by Mari Schuh.
Description: Minneapolis, MN : Jump!, Inc., [2018]
Series: Plant power
Includes bibliographical references and index.
Identifiers: LCCN 2017058944 (print)
LCCN 2017055705 (ebook)
ISBN 9781624968914 (ebook)
ISBN 9781624968891 (hardcover : alk. paper)
ISBN 9781624968907 (pbk.)
Subjects: LCSH: Plant defenses–Juvenile literature. Thorns–Juvenile literature.
Classification: LCC QK921 (print)
LCC QK921 .S38 2018 (ebook) | DDC 581.4/7–dc23
LC record available at https://lccn.loc.gov/2017058944

Editor: Jenna Trnka
Book Designer: Molly Ballanger

Photo Credits: Butterfly Hunter/Shutterstock, cover; jopelka/Shutterstock, 1; Evgeni_S/Shutterstock, 3; GotziLA STOCK/Shutterstock, 4; Phuongphoto/Dreamstime, 5; Danita Delimont/Getty, 6-7; Garden World Images/Alamy, 8-9; DmitryKomarov/Shutterstock, 10-11; AndreyUG/Shutterstock, 12; Oleg Kovtun Hydrobio/Shutterstock, 13; Sirirak Kaewgorn/Dreamstime, 14-15; Yulia Plekhanova/Shutterstock, 16; Bildagentur Zoonar GmbH/Shutterstock, 17; All for you friend/Shutterstock, 18-19; cpaulfell/Shutterstock, 20-21; Erika Kirkpatrick/Shutterstock, 23.

Printed in the United States of America at Corporate Graphics in North Mankato, Minnesota.

TABLE OF CONTENTS

CHAPTER 1
Thorns and Spines 4

CHAPTER 2
Spiny Cacti 12

CHAPTER 3
Prickly Trees 16

ACTIVITIES & TOOLS
Try This! 22
Glossary 23
Index 24
To Learn More 24

THORNS AND SPINES

Bright red flowers **bloom** among green leaves. What a nice plant! But flowers aren't all this plant has.

It is called a crown of thorns. And for a good reason. The **stem** and **branches** are covered with sharp **spines**. The one-inch (2.5-centimeter) spines poke anything that gets too close.

spine

Plants like the crown of thorns are very **prickly**. Why? Plants cannot move. Spines serve as a **defense**. Against what? **Predators**, such as birds, that try to eat the plant.

DID YOU KNOW?

A crown of thorns plant can sprawl more than 6 feet (1.8 meters). That is longer than an adult bicycle!

Spines stick straight up on the porcupine tomato plant. They are bright orange. There is almost no way to miss them. The stems and leaves are covered with these sharp, dangerous spines. Ouch! They are also a warning that this plant has **poison**. Stay away!

TAKE A LOOK!

Most plants have the same main parts. Prickly plants, such as rose bushes, also have prickles. These help keep hungry **herbivores** away.

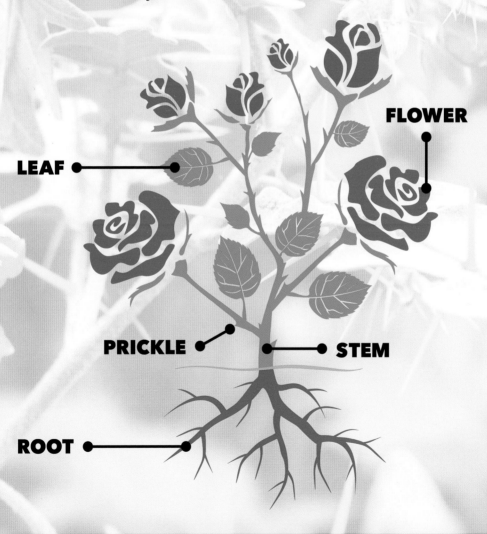

LEAF

FLOWER

PRICKLE

STEM

ROOT

Oregon grape holly might not look very prickly. But look closer. This prickly plant has sharp spines on the edges of its leaves. How sharp? They can **pierce** through thick skin. Animals looking for a meal learn a painful lesson. They need to fill their bellies elsewhere.

CHAPTER 2

SPINY CACTI

Cacti are some of the best known prickly plants. Almost all cacti have spines or barbed **bristles**.

Some cacti are completely covered in spines. It wouldn't be any fun to get caught in this prickly web!

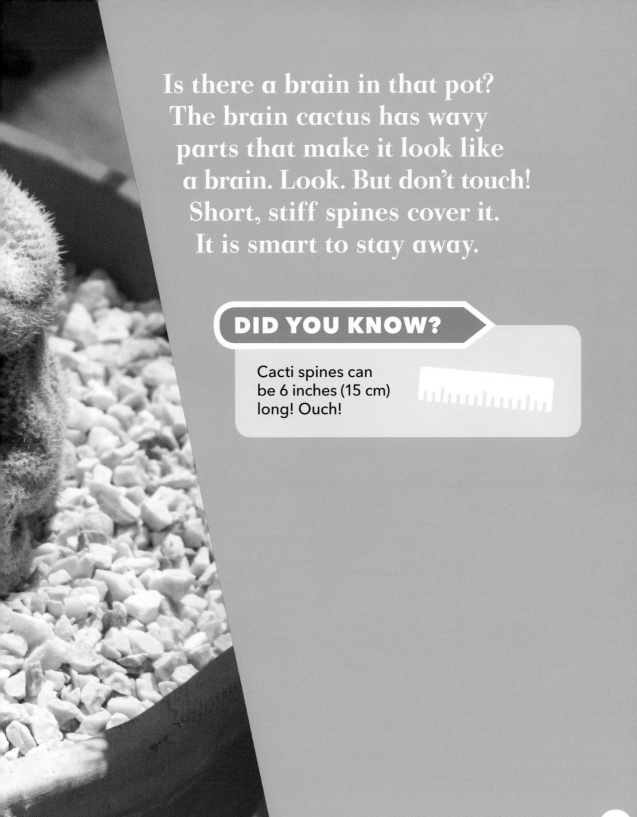

Is there a brain in that pot?
The brain cactus has wavy
parts that make it look like
a brain. Look. But don't touch!
Short, stiff spines cover it.
It is smart to stay away.

DID YOU KNOW?

Cacti spines can
be 6 inches (15 cm)
long! Ouch!

CHAPTER 3

PRICKLY TREES

Trees can be fun to climb. But you may not want to climb the floss-silk tree. Why? Large spines cover the trunk.

They also cover the branches. Hungry animals have a hard time reaching the tree's flowers and fruit without getting hurt. It is best to avoid this prickly tree!

thorn

Hungry animals might want to chomp on a honey locust tree's leaves. But if they are smart, they will find another plant to nibble and chew. The big, sharp thorns on these trees can be 12 inches (30 cm) long. That is as long as a ruler!

The thorns on the whistling thorn tree protect against large animals. Like what? Giraffes and antelopes. Even hungry elephants! The thorns are long and sharp.

Whistling thorn trees are home to busy little ants. How? Some thorns have round, **hollow** bases. The ants chew holes in the bases to get inside.

Prickly plants around the world poke to protect themselves. Where have you seen prickly plants?

base

ACTIVITIES & TOOLS

PRICKLY CACTUS

Create your own cactus to see how spines help protect this plant.

What You Need:
- cucumber
- toothpicks
- paper plate

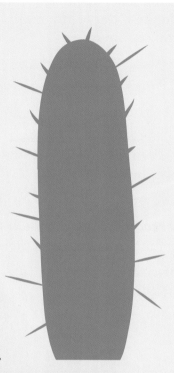

1. With an adult's help, cut one end off of the cucumber.

2. Placing the flat end on the plate, stand the cucumber up straight.

3. Carefully push toothpicks in all around the cucumber. You can make them as long or as short as you'd like. If you want them shorter, push them in farther.

4. After you are done placing the toothpicks, try touching the cucumber with your finger. Do the spines poke you? How does this activity help you see how cacti protect themselves from hungry predators?

GLOSSARY

bloom: To produce flowers.

branches: The parts of plants that grow out of the main trunk or bough.

bristles: Short, stiff hairs on plants or animals.

defense: The ability to protect from harm or attack.

herbivores: Animals that eat only plants.

hollow: Empty on the inside.

pierce: To make a hole or opening in or through an object.

poison: A substance that can kill or harm.

predators: Living things that get food by killing and eating other living things.

prickly: Having small, sharp points.

spines: Hard, sharp, pointed growths on plants or trees.

stem: The part of a plant from which leaves and flowers grow.

INDEX

animals 10, 17, 19, 20

bases 20

brain cactus 15

branches 5, 17

bristles 12

cacti 12, 13, 15

crown of thorns 4, 5, 6

defense 6

floss-silk tree 16, 17

flowers 4, 9, 17

fruit 17

herbivores 9

honey locust tree 19

leaves 4, 8, 9, 10, 19

Oregon grape holly 10

poison 8

porcupine tomato plant 8

predators 6

rose bushes 9

spines 5, 6, 8, 10, 12, 13, 15, 16

stem 5, 8, 9

thorns 19, 20

trunk 16

whistling thorn tree 20

TO LEARN MORE

Learning more is as easy as 1, 2, 3.

1) Go to www.factsurfer.com
2) Enter "pricklyplants" into the search box.
3) Click the "Surf" button to see a list of websites.

With factsurfer, finding more information is just a click away.